CCSS **Genre** Nonfiction

Essential Question

How can you find your way around?

by Francine Thompson

Many people use maps.
Maps help us find places.

Let's visit a park! Maps
will help us get around.

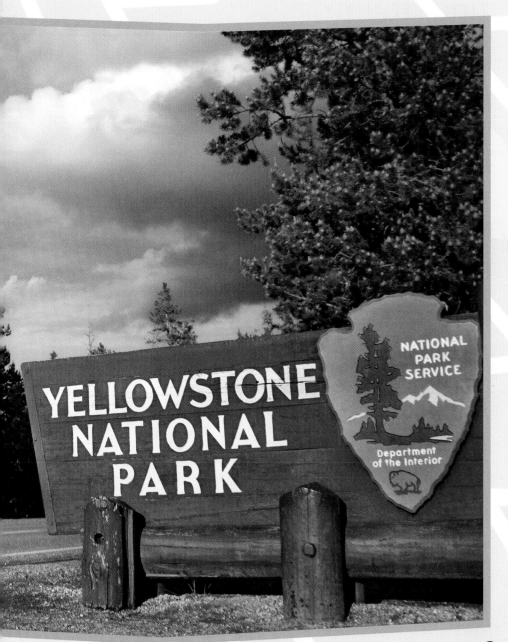

This park has many animals. How can we find them?

deer

beaver

eagle

The map shows where
the animals live. Let's visit
the deer first.

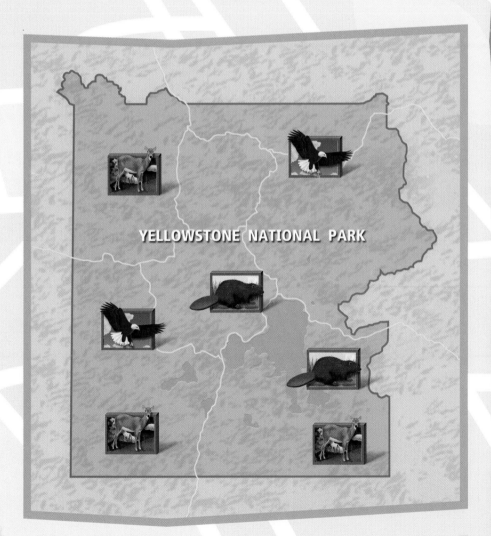

YELLOWSTONE NATIONAL PARK

The park has trails. How do we know where they are?

This map shows trails. Let's walk by the pond.

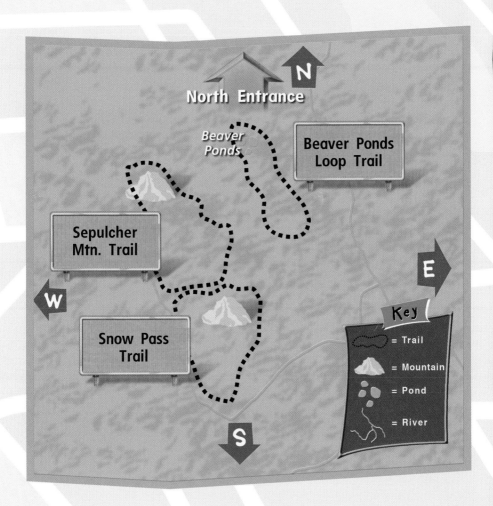

The park has picnic areas.
How can we find them?

This map has picnic areas.
Let's choose a place.

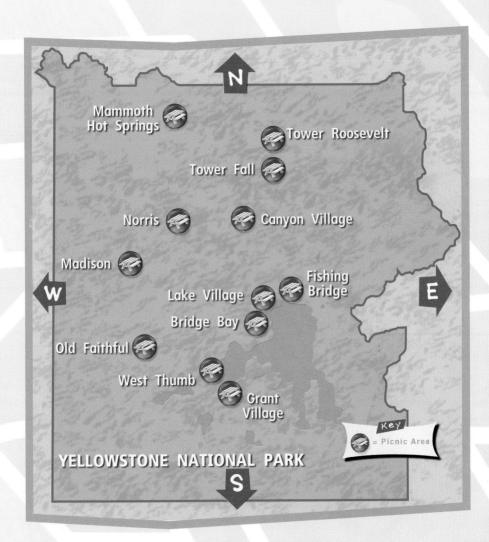

Illustration: Rob Schuster

It's time to go home.
How do we find the
way out?

This map shows the way out. We had fun using maps!

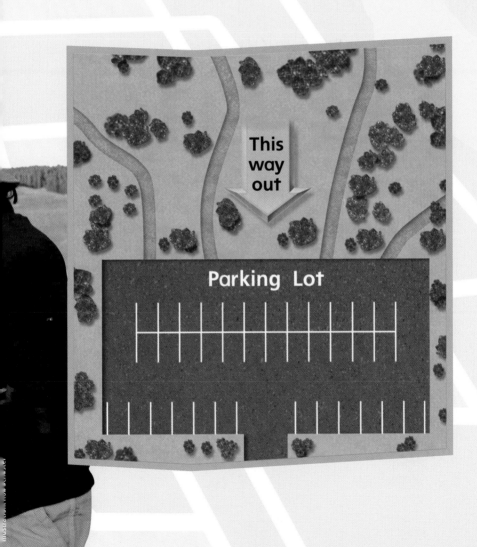

This
way
out

Parking Lot

Respond to
Reading

Retell

Main Topic		
Detail	Detail	Detail

Use your own words to retell details in *How Maps Help.*

Text Evidence

1. What is the main topic of this book? Main Topic and Key Details

2. Look at page 7. What does this map show? Main Topic and Key Details

3. How do you know that *How Maps Help* is nonfiction? Genre

Compare Texts
How do we use maps?

On the Map

We are at the bus stop. We are on A Street. Let's take the bus to E Street. Look at the bus map. Where is E Street?

Let's go!

F Street

E Street

D Street

C Street

B Street

A Street

Main Street

Make Connections

Look at both selections. How do maps help? Text to Text

Focus on
Social Studies

Purpose To make a map of your classroom

What to Do

Step 1 Look around your classroom. Where is your desk? Where are the windows? Where is the door?

Step 2 Draw a map of your classroom. Label your desk.

Step 3 Share your map with the class.